GRAMMAR WORKBOOK 1
SERIES EDITORS
JoAnn (Jodi) Crandall
Joan Kang Shin

Australia • Brazil • Mexico • Singapore • United Kingdom • United States

Unit 1

1 **Unscramble.** Write a question.

1. c c k o l _____clock_____ _____Is it a clock_____?

2. p a m _____ _____?

3. n l c p e i _____ _____?

4. n e p _____ _____?

2 **Look and read.** Write the answer.

1.  Is it a clock? _____Yes, it is_____.

2. Is it a crayon? _____.

3.  Is it a map? _____.

4. Is it a board? _____.

5. Is it a computer? _____.

3 **Write.** Look at Activity 2.

1. ___It's a clock___ .

2. _____ .

3. _____ .

4. _____ .

5. _____ .

4 **Look and write.**

1. ● ___It's a circle___ .

2. ★ _____ .

3. ▲ _____ .

4. ■ _____ .

5 **Draw and write.** Draw a picture of your classroom. Write 2 questions and 2 answers.

_____

_____

_____

_____

1 Read and match. Draw a line.

1. Is it a   a. it?

2. It's an   b. picture?

3. What color   c. is it?

4. What is   d. papers?

5. How many   e. eraser.

2 Read. Write *What*, *What's*, or *How*.

1. _____ your name?   I'm Sandy.

2. _____ color is it?   It's purple.

3. _____ many pictures?   Six.

4. _____ is it?   It's a chair.

3 Read and write. Complete the questions.

1. ____What is it____?   It's a book.

2. _____?   It's black.

3. _____ chairs?   Five.

4. _____ a board?   No, it's a picture.

4 Look and write.

1.  How many chairs _____?

   Three _____.

2. 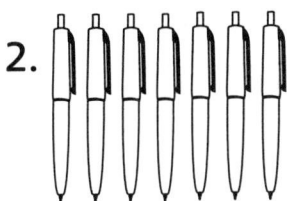 _____?

   _____.

3. _____?

   _____.

4. _____?

   _____.

5 Write. Color the picture. Answer the questions.

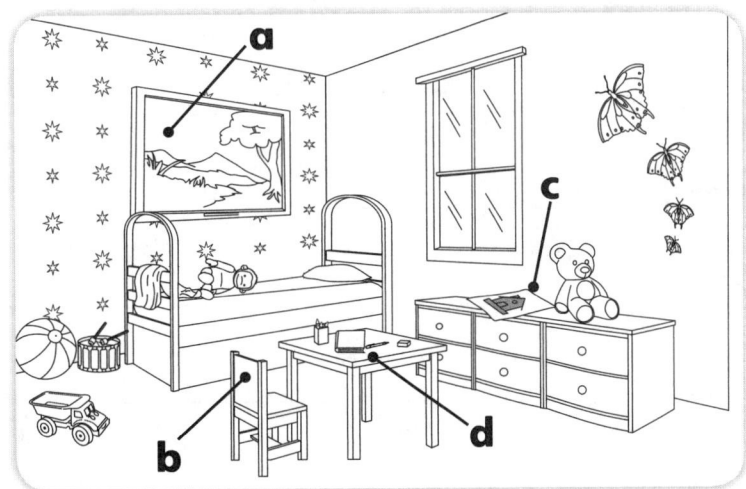

1. Look at **a**. What is it?

   _____.

2. Look at **b**. What color is it?

   _____.

3. Look at **c**. What is it?

   _____.

4. Look at **d**. What color is it?

   _____.

Unit 2

1 **Read.** Circle the words.

1. **What / Is** it a river?   Yes, it **is / are**.

2. What **is / are** it?   It **'s** / **are** a bird.

3. What **is / are** they?   They **is / are** frogs.

4. **What / How** are they?   **It's / They're** rocks.

2 **Read.** Rewrite the sentences.

1. It is a butterfly. <u>It's a butterfly</u>   .

2. They are rocks. _____.

3. It is a stick. _____.

4. They are trees. _____.

3 **Look.** Write questions.

1. <u>What is it</u> ?

2. _____ ?

3. _____ ?

4. _____ ?

5. _____ ?

4 **Look.** Answer the questions in Activity 3. Use the picture.

1. <u>It's a mountain</u> .

2. _____ .

3. _____ .

4. _____ .

5. _____ .

5 **Look and write.** Write 2 questions and 2 answers about the picture on p. 6.

_____ ?   _____ ?

_____ .   _____ .

1 **Read.** Circle the letter.

1. The clouds are _____ the sky.   a. is   b. on   c. in

2. The trees _____ in the grass.   a. is   b. are   c. on

3. The rainbow _____ in the sky.   a. is   b. on   c. are

4. Where _____ the parrots?   a. is   b. in   c. are

5. The monkey is _____ the rock.   a. in   b. are   c. on

6. Where _____ the elephant?   a. is   b. are   c. in

2 **Look.** Write *in* or *on*.

1. The bird is _____ the tree.   3. The star is _____ the sky.

2. The rocks are _____ the river.   4. The bird is _____ the stick.

8

3 **Look and write.**

1. Where is the butterfly?

2. _____

3. _____

4. _____

4 **Write.** Answer the questions in Activity 3.

1. It's on the grass. _____

2. _____

3. _____

4. _____

5 **Look and write.** Look outside. Write 3 questions and answers about what you see.

Where's the sun? It's in the sky. _____

_____

_____

_____

Unit 3

> **GRAMMAR**
>
> **Do** you **have** any brothers or sisters? Yes, I do.
>
> How many grandmothers **do** you **have**? I **have** two grandmothers.   **don't** =
>
> How many brothers **do** you **have**? I **don't have** any brothers.   do not

1 **Write.** Unscramble the sentences.

1. brother / have / a / I / big

   <u>I have a big brother</u>.

2. have / sister / a / I / baby

   _____.

3. a / don't / brother / I / have

   _____.

4. parents / I / two / have

   _____.

2 **Read and write.** Give answers that are true for you.

1. <u>Do you have</u> _____ any sisters?

   _____.

2. How many parents _____?

   _____.

3. How many grandfathers _____?

   _____.

4. _____ any brothers?

   _____.

3 Look and write.

1. sister <u>I don't have any sisters</u>_____.

2. mother _____.

3. father _____.

4. brother _____.

5. grandfather _____.

4 Write. Write questions to ask a friend about family. Use the words in the box.

> (baby/big) brother   (baby/big) sister   grandfather/grandmother

1. <u>Do you have a baby sister</u>_____?

2. _____?

3. _____?

4. _____?

5 Write. Write 2 sentences about your family. Use *have.*

_____

_____

1 **Look and write.**

1. Who's he?   2. _____   3. _____

2 **Look and write.** Imagine this is your family.

1.    Who's he? __He's my baby brother__. He's two.

2.   Who's she? _____. She's short.

3.   Who's he? _____. He's old.

4.    Who's she? _____. She's tall.

3 **Write.** Write questions and answers.

1. <u>Who's he</u> _____?

   <u>He's my big brother. He's tall</u> _____. (tall)

2. _____?

   _____. (young)

3. _____?

   _____. (ten)

4. _____?

   _____. (small)

4 **Draw and write.** Draw 2 people in your family. Then write about them. Use the words in the box.

| old | short | tall | young |

_____

_____

_____

_____

1 Read and match. Draw a line.

1. Who's he?

2. Where is the bird?

3. What are they?

4. What color is it?

5. What is it?

6. Is it a bird?

7. How many books?

a. Three.

b. It's in the sky.

c. He's my grandfather.

d. They're birds.

e. It's a bird.

f. No, it isn't. It's a frog.

g. It's blue.

2 Look and write. Complete the questions.

1. _____ a book?

2. What color _____?

3. _____ she?

4. What _____?

5. _____ the tree?

6. How many brothers _____?

14

3 **Write.** Answer the questions in Activity 2.

1. _____ .   4. _____ .

2. _____ .   5. _____ .

3. _____ .   6. _____ .

4 **Look and write.**

1.

The birds _____ .

2.

_____ the grass.

3.

_____ .

4.

_____ .

5 **Look and color.** Write sentences.

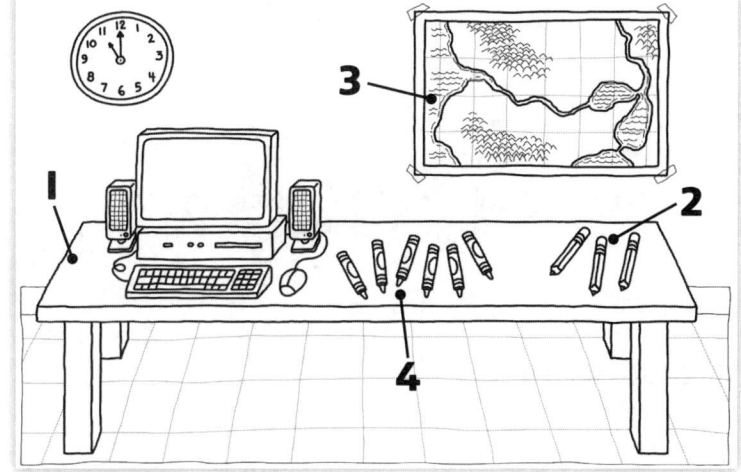

1. It's yellow _____ .

2. _____ .

3. _____ .

4. _____ .

Unit 4

1 **Read.** Look at your house. (Circle) the letter.

 1. Is there a sofa in the bedroom?

   a. Yes, there is.   b. No, there isn't.

 2. Is there a clock in the kitchen?

   a. Yes, there is.   b. No, there isn't.

 3. Is there a chair in the living room?

   a. Yes, there is.   b. No, there isn't.

 4. Is there a lamp in the dining room?

   a. Yes, there is.   b. No, there isn't.

2 **Look and write.**

 1. ___Is there___ a sofa in the

   bedroom? ___No, there isn't___.

 2. _____ a clock in the

   bedroom? _____.

 3. _____ a bed in the bedroom? _____.

 4. _____ a chair in the bedroom? _____.

3 **Look.** Write questions.

1. <u>Is there a bed in the</u>
   <u>bedroom</u> ?

2. _____
   _____ ?

3. _____
   _____ ?

4. _____
   _____ ?

4 **Write.** Answer your questions from Activity 3.

1. <u>Yes, there is</u> .

2. _____ .

3. _____ .

4. _____ .

5 **Draw and write.** Draw your living room. Write 2 questions and answers.

_____

_____

_____

_____

GRAMMAR

Where's your grandmother?   She's in the bedroom.   **'s sleeping** =
                            She**'s sleeping**.   is sleeping

Where's your grandfather?   He's in the dining room.   **'s reading** =
                            He**'s reading**.   is reading

---

1 **Look and read.** (Circle) **the word.**

1.    **She / She's**
   eating.

3.    **He's / He**
   taking a bath.

2.    She's
   sleeping /
   sleep.

4.    He's
   watching /
   watch TV.

---

2 **Write.** Rewrite the sentences. Use 's.

1. He is drawing. __He's drawing_____.

2. She is singing. _____.

3. The baby is sleeping in the bedroom. _____

_____.

4. My brother is watching TV in the living room. _____

_____.

3 Look and write.

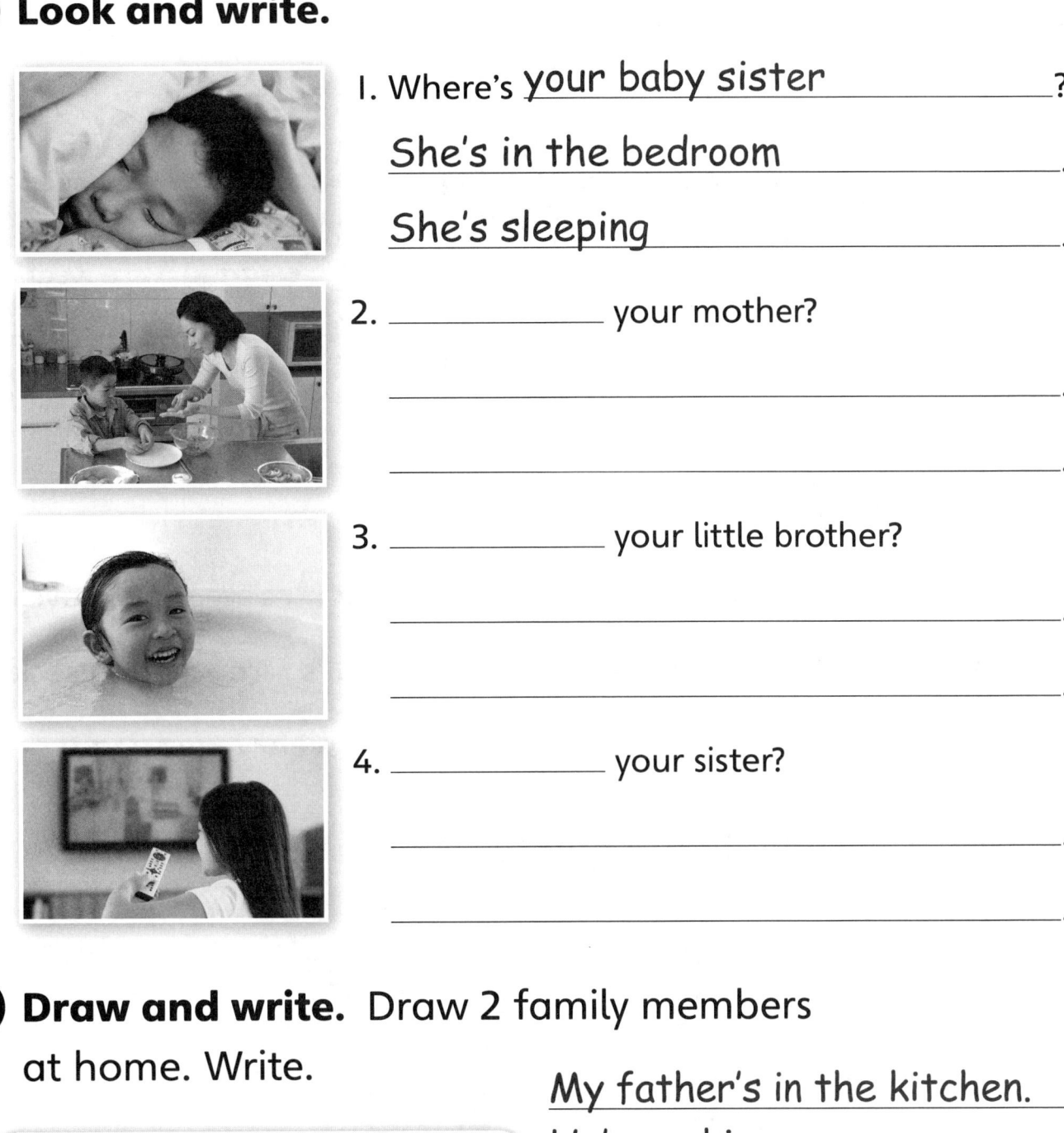

1. Where's <u>your baby sister</u> ____ ?

<u>She's in the bedroom</u> ____ .

<u>She's sleeping</u> ____ .

2. ____ your mother?

____ .

____ .

3. ____ your little brother?

____ .

____ .

4. ____ your sister?

____ .

____ .

4 Draw and write. Draw 2 family members at home. Write.

<u>My father's in the kitchen.</u>
<u>He's cooking.</u>

____

____

____

____

____

Unit 5

GRAMMAR

What **are** you **wearing**?   **I'm wearing** green socks.   **'m wearing** = am wearing

You**'re wearing** a red jacket.   **'re wearing** = are wearing

What **is** he **wearing**?   My father**'s wearing** a shirt.   **'s wearing** = is wearing

1 **Read.** Circle.

1. What **is / are** she wearing?

2. What **is / are** you wearing?

3. **She's / She** wearing a red dress.

4. I **'m / 're** wearing gloves.

5. You **'s / 're** wearing socks.

6. I'm **wear / wearing** a skirt.

2 **Write.** Complete the questions on p. 21.

You

1. What _____ your mother _____?

2. What _____ your brother _____?

3. What _____ your father _____?

4. What _____ you _____?

③ Color and write. Use Activity 2.

1. _____.

2. _____.

3. _____.

4. _____.

④ Look and write.

1. What is he wearing? He's wearing pants. He's wearing a shirt.

3. _____

_____

_____

2. _____

_____

_____

You

_____

4. _____

_____

_____

_____

1 **Look and read.** Circle the words. Then match.

1. What's **that / those**?   a. **That / Those** are my gloves.

2. What are **that / those**?   b. **That's / Those** my hat.

3. What **'s / are** that?   c. **That's / Those** my skirt.

4. What **is / are** those?   d. **That's / Those are** my socks.

5. **What's / What are** that?   e. That **'s / are** my T-shirt.

2 **Write.**

1. What's that _____? That's my blue dress.

2. _____? Those are my red gloves.

3. _____? Those are my black shoes.

4. _____? That's my white shirt.

5. _____? Those are my brown pants.

3 **Look and write.** Ask and answer questions.

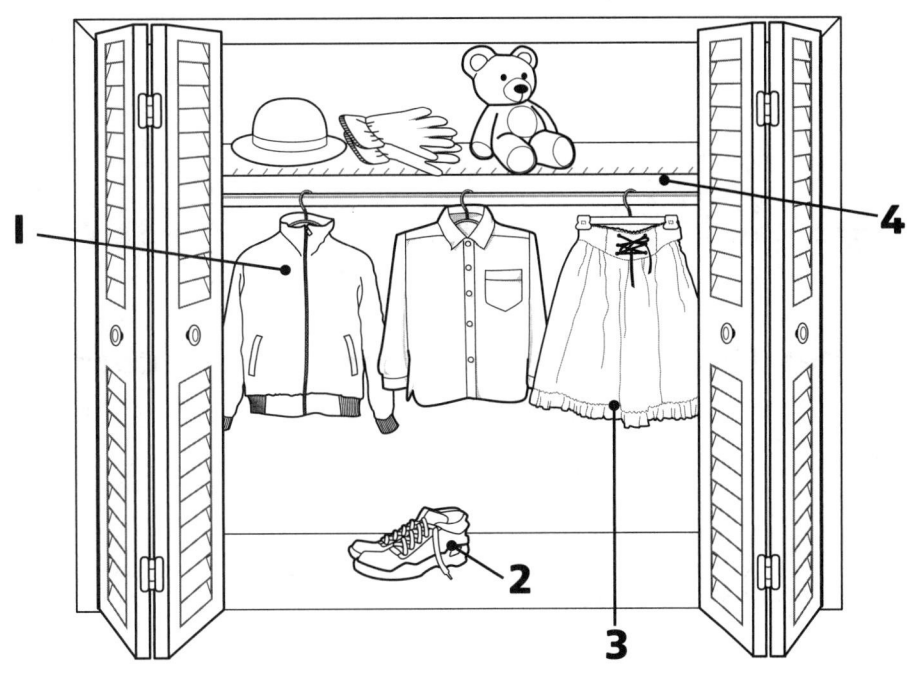

1. <u>What's that</u> ? <u>That's my jacket</u> .

2. _____ ? _____ .

3. _____ ? _____ .

4. _____ ? _____ .

4 **Draw and write.** Draw and color a picture of your clothes. Choose 3 things. Write sentences.

_____

_____

_____

_____

Unit 6

GRAMMAR

Do you **want** a bike?	Yes, I **do**.	
Do you **want** a truck?	No, I **don't**.	**don't** = do not
Does he **want** a bike?	Yes, he **does**.	
Does she **want** a truck?	No, she **doesn't**. She **wants** a kite.	**doesn't** = does not

1 **Read.** Circle the words.

1. **Do / Does** you want a top? Yes, I **do / does**.

2. **Do / Does** he want a train? Yes, he **do / does**.

3. **Do / Does** she want a bike? Yes, she **does / doesn't**.

4. Do you **want / wants** a ball? No, I **don't / do**.

2 **Read and write.**

1. Does she __want__ a kite?

2. _____ you want a truck?

3. He _____ a puppet.

4. Does your brother _____ a top?

5. Do you _____ a train?

6. I _____ a bike.

3 **Read and write.** Answer the questions.

1. Do you want a computer? _____.

2. Do you want a big car? _____.

3. Do you want a baby sister? _____.

4. Do you want a bike? _____.

4 **Look and write.**

1. she / ☹ Does she want a train _____?

No, she doesn't _____.

2. he / ☺ _____?

_____.

3. he / ☹ _____?

_____.

4. she / ☺ _____?

_____.

5 **Draw and write.** Draw 2 toys. Ask and answer questions with *want*.

_____?

_____.

_____?

_____.

1 **Read.** Circle the words.

1. Is **this / these** your top?

   No, it **isn't / aren't**.

   It's / They're Juan's top.

2. Are these her **toy / toys**?

   No, they **aren't / isn't**.

   They're / It's my toys.

3. Are **this / these** your balls?

   Yes, **it / they** are.

4. **Are / Is** this your doll?

   No, **it / they** isn't.

   It's her **doll / dolls**.

2 **Read and write.** Complete the sentences.

1. _____ your robot?

   Yes, it _____.

2. _____ your puzzles?

   No, they _____. _____ Bob's puzzles.

3. _____ her teddy bear?

   No, it _____.

4. _____ your dolls?

   Yes, they _____.

26

3 **Look and write.** Ask questions. Follow the model.

1. **Paolo's**

Is this your truck?
_____

2. **Carmen's**
_____
_____

3. **Maya's**
_____
_____

4. **Ava's**
_____
_____

4 **Write.** Answer the questions in Activity 3.

1. No, it isn't. It's Paolo's truck. _____

2. _____

3. _____

4. _____

5 **Write.** Write a conversation between friends about toys. Use the words in the box.

| aren't | isn't | these | this |

_____

_____

_____

_____

1 Read and match. (Circle) the words. Draw a line.

1. What's **that / those**?

2. Is **this / there** a TV in the living room?

3. **Where's / Where** your baby brother?

4. **Is this / Are these** your toy?

5. **Does / Do** she want a doll?

a. He's in the bedroom. He's **sleep / sleeping**.

b. No, she **does / doesn't**.

c. No, **it's / it isn't**.

d. Yes, **there / there is**.

e. **That's / Those are** my game.

2 Look and write. Complete the questions and answers.

1. _____? That's a photo of my family.

2. Is this your hat? _____.

3. What's that? _____.

4. _____? Yes, I do. I want a chair.

5. _____? I'm wearing a shirt.

28

3 Read and write.

1. Do you want a hat? 🙂 _____.

2. Do you want brown shoes? 🙁 _____.

3. _____? 🙁 _____.
   They're my sister's gloves.

4. Does your mother want _____? 🙂
   _____. She wants a computer.

4 Draw and write. Draw 2 people in the house. Write about them.

My mother's in the living room.
She's wearing pants and a shirt.
She's watching TV.

_____

_____

_____

_____

_____

_____

_____

5 Write. Where are you? What are you wearing? Write sentences.

_____

_____

Unit 7

GRAMMAR

I have brown hair. **My** hair is brown.

You have brown hair. **Your** hair is brown.

Nick has brown hair. **His** hair is brown.

Nancy has green eyes. **Her** eyes are green.

You and I have brown eyes. **Our** eyes are brown.

You and Nick have brown hair. **Your** hair is brown.

Nick and Nancy have green eyes. **Their** eyes are green.

1 **Look and read.** Circle the word.

1. **His / Your** hair is black.

2. **His / Their** hair is black.

3. **Her / Their** hair is black.

4. **My / Our** hair is black.

   Your / My eyes are black, too!

5. This is my family.

   Our / Your hair is black.

4 You

2 **Read and write.** Use the words.

1. hair / short _Her hair is short_____ .

   eyes / black _____ .

2. hair / short _____ .

3. hair / black _____ .

   eyes / black / too _____

   _____ .

3 **Read.** Rewrite the sentences.

1. I have short hair. <u>My hair is short</u>_____.

2. My father has big ears. _____.

3. You have small hands. _____.

4. My grandmother and grandfather have white hair.

_____.

5. My little sister has short legs. _____.

6. My baby brother has a small mouth. _____.

4 **Look and write.** Use *her*, *his*, *my*, and *your*.

1. _____. (hair)   2. _____. (hand)

_____. (eyes)   _____. (nose)

5 **Write.** Find a photo of friends or family members. Put it here. Write 4 sentences about it.

Put photo here

_____

_____

_____

_____

1 **Read and match.** Draw a line.

1. I can walk on my hands.   a. He has strong arms.

2. I can jump on one foot.   b. She has strong legs.

3. She can run and jump.   c. I have strong arms.

4. He can walk on his hands, too.   d. I have strong legs.

2 **Write.** Unscramble the words.

1. I / jump / can _____.

2. she / clean / can _____.

3. watch / he / can / TV _____.

4. baby / can / my / sister / eat _____.

5. run / you / can _____?

3 **Look and write.** Write 3 sentences. Use *can*.

She can jump. _____

_____

_____

_____

4 **Look and write.** Write questions and answers. See p. 7 in your Student Book.

1. <u>Can you draw</u> _____ ?

   <u>Yes, I can</u> _____ .

2. _____ ?

   _____ .

3. _____ ?

   _____ .

4. _____ ?

   _____ .

5 **Write.** Write 4 sentences about your friends or family. Use *can*.

<u>My father can cook.</u> _____

_____

_____

_____

_____

Unit 8

GRAMMAR

Do you **like** cookies?	Yes, I **do**. I **like** cookies.
Do you **like** soup?	No, I **don't**. I **don't like** soup.
Does he **like** bananas?	Yes, he **does**. He **likes** bananas.
Does she **like** chicken?	No, she **doesn't**. She **doesn't like** chicken.

don't = do not

doesn't = does not

1 **Read.** Circle your answer.

1. Do you like fish?

   a. Yes, I do.   b. No, I don't.

2. Do you like apples?

   a. Yes, I do.   b. No, I don't.

3. Do you like chicken?

   a. Yes, I do.   b. No, I don't.

4. Do you like rice?

   a. Yes, I do.   b. No, I don't.

5. Do you like sandwiches?

   a. Yes, I do.   b. No, I don't.

2 **Read.** Write your answer.

1. Do you like computers? _____.

2. Do you like kites? _____.

3. Do you like robots? _____.

4. Do you like puzzles? _____.

3 **Read and write.**

1. _Does_ he like sandwiches? No, he _doesn't_. He doesn't like sandwiches.

2. _____ you like oranges? Yes, I _____. I like oranges.

3. Does she _____ cookies? Yes, she does. She _____ cookies.

4. Do you _____ soup? No, I don't. I _____ like soup.

5. _____ she _____ eggs? No, she _____ like eggs.

4 **Read.** Write answers that are true for you.

1. Do you want a cookie? _No, I don't. I don't like cookies._

2. Do you want some chicken? _____

3. Do you want an apple? _____

4. Do you want some rice? _____

5 **Look and write.** Write about people in your family.

1. grandfather _Does your grandfather like eggs?_
   No, he doesn't. He likes chicken.

2. mother _____

3. brother/sister _____

4. grandmother _____

1 **Write.** Make 2 lists.

apple	arm
banana	computer
ear	egg
eraser	fish
mouth	tree

a	an
	apple

2 **Read.** Write *a* or *an*.

1. Is it _____ pencil? No, it isn't. It's _____ table.

2. Is it _____ eraser? Yes, it is!

3. Is there _____ sofa in the living room? No, but there's _____ chair.

4. Does he want _____ apple? No. He wants _____ cookie.

5. There's _____ yellow butterfly. It's not _____ orange butterfly.

3 **Look and write.** Complete the sentences.

1. There is a ___girl___, an _____,
   a _____, and an _____.

2. There isn't an _____, a
   _____, a _____, and an
   _____.

4 Look and write.

1. _an orange_

2. _____

3. _____

4. _____

5. _____

6. _____

7. _____

8. _____

5 Write. Complete the sentences. Use all of the words.

board	chair	egg	eraser
old toy	orange	table	umbrella

1. In my classroom, there _isn't an orange._____

   _There is a board._____

2. In my living room, there _____

   _____

3. In my kitchen, there _____

   _____

4. In my bedroom, there _____

   _____

Unit 9

GRAMMAR

What **are** the frogs **doing**?	They'**re jumping**.	**They're** = They are
Are they **eating**?	Yes, they **are**.	
Are they **climbing**?	No, they **aren't**.	**aren't** = are not

1 **Write.**

1. sleep <u>They're sleeping</u>.   4. jump _____.

2. clean _____.   5. sing _____.

3. walk _____.   6. eat _____.

2 **Read and write.**

1. What _____ the cats doing?

2. _____ they running? Yes, they _____.

3. What are the sheep _____?

4. Are _____ jumping? No, they _____.

5. They _____ sleeping.

3 **Look and write.** Use the picture on p. 38.

1. Are the cows sleeping? _____.

2. What are the cats doing? _____.

3. Are the goats jumping? _____.

4. What are the horses doing? _____.

5. Are the goats eating? _____.

4 **Look.** Write questions.

1. _____? They're eating.

2. _____? Yes, they are. They're eating.

3. _____? They're walking.

4. _____? They're sleeping.

5. _____? Yes, they are. They're jumping.

5 **Look and write.** Open your Student Book to pp. 146–147. Write 3 questions and answers about the picture.

What are the cats doing? They're sleeping.

_____

_____

_____

GRAMMAR

Do you **want to ride** the horse? No, I don't. │ **don't** = do not

Does he **want to ride** the horse? No, he doesn't. │ **doesn't** = does not

What **do** you **want to do**? I **want to see** the turtle.

What **does** Bao **want to do**? He **wants to see** the goats.

1 **Read. Circle the answer.**

1. Do you **want / want to** ride a horse?

2. **Do / Does** she want to swim?

3. **Do / Does** you want to climb a tree?

4. What **do / does** your brother want to do?

5. What **do / does** you want to do?

6. What does your father **want / wanting** to do?

2 **Read and write.**

1. I _____ to see the cat.

2. _____ you want to see the cow?

3. What _____ Mei want to do?

4. What does Jian _____ to do?

5. He _____ to see the duck.

6. _____ she want to see the goat? No, she _____.

7. What _____ you _____ to do? I want to see the dog.

8. Do you _____ to see the sheep? No, I _____.

3 **Read.** Write questions.

1. _____?

   I want to fly in the sky.

2. _____?

   She wants to ride a bike.

3. _____?

   She wants to crawl on the grass.

4. _____?

   No, he doesn't. My father wants to read.

5. _____?

   No, I don't. I don't like cats.

4 **Write.** Write questions.

> ~~in your kitchen~~   in your living room
> at school   with your friends   with your parents

1. What do you want to do in your kitchen? _____

2. _____

3. _____

4. _____

5. _____

5 **Read and write.** Answer the questions in Activity 4.

1. I want to cook. _____

2. _____

3. _____

4. _____

5. _____

1 Read and match. Circle the words. Then draw a line.

1. Do you **like / likes** turtles?

2. What are the sheep **do / doing**?

3. **Is / Are** the dogs sleeping?

4. What does Eve **want / wants** to do?

5. **Does / Do** he like cats?

a. They **'re / 's** running.

b. She **want / wants** to cook.

c. Yes, he **do / does**.

d. No, they **are / aren't**.

e. Yes, I **do / does**.

2 Look and write.

1.

an apple

2.

_____

3.

_____

4.

_____

5.

_____

6.

_____

3 Look and write. What can they do?

You

1. _____.

2. _____.

3. _____.

4. _____.

4 **Look and write.** Use the picture from Activity 3.

1. What color is the girl's hair? _____.

2. What color are the boy's pants? _____.

3. What are the sheep doing? _____.

4. What does the girl want to do? _____.

5. Does the boy like climbing? _____.

5 **Read.** Write questions.

1. _____?

Yes, I do. I like soup very much.

2. _____?

They're jumping.

3. _____?

My mother wants to clean.

4. _____?

No, they aren't cooking. They're eating.

5. _____?

No, I don't. I don't want to run.

6 **Write.** Write about you. Use *can*, *like*, and *want*.

_____

_____

_____

_____

1 Read. Circle.

1. **a / an** apple
2. **a / an** sheep

3. **a / an** top
4. **a / an** eye

5. **a / an** arm
6. **a / an** eraser

2 Read and write.

1. My mother's hair is brown. <u>Her hair is brown.</u>

2. My grandfather's gloves are red. _____

3. I have a truck. It's orange. _____

4. You have a pencil. It's green. _____

3 Look and write.

1. Who's she? _____

   _____

2. What is it? _____

3. _____?
   Yes, it is.

4. What's that? _____

5. Where is the top? _____

   _____

6. _____? No, it isn't. It's my sister's train.

7. _____? I'm wearing a shirt.

44

4 Read and write.

1. Does your brother want a cat? 🙁 _____

2. Is this Dana's doll? 🙁 _____

3. Are these our toys? 🙂 _____

4. Do you want to eat chicken? 🙂 _____

5 Read and write.

1. Do you want crayons? _____

2. Do you like milk? _____

3. Do you want to ride a horse? _____

4. What are you wearing? _____

5. How many grandmothers do you have? _____

6 Read and write. Ask questions.

1. _____ That's my bike.

2. _____ No, he doesn't want a cookie.

3. _____ Yes, I do. I like turtles.

4. _____ Yes, I do. I want a computer.

5. _____ He's in the kitchen. He's cooking.

6. _____ I have two books.

7. _____ He's my brother.

7 **Look and write.** Use the words.

1. What color is the bird? _____ (color)

   It's white. _____ (white)

2. _____ (it)

   _____ (river)

3. _____ (many)

   _____ (three)

4. _____ (doing)

   _____ (jumping)

8 **Write.** Write 4 sentences about you. Use the words in the box.

| can | like | my | want (to) | wearing |

_____

_____

_____

_____

GAME

Read and write. Complete the sentences. Match letters and shapes.

1. ___ ___ ___ is she? ___ ___ ___ is my ___ ___ ___ ___ sister.

2. Is ___ ___ ___ ___ ___ a ___ ___ ___ ___ in the bedroom?

    Yes, there is. The lamp is next to the bed.

3. Do you want a pen? ___ ___ ___, I do.

4. ___ ___ ___ these ___ ___ ___ ___ shoes? Yes, they are my shoes.

5. What does she ___ ___ ___ ___ to do? She wants to sleep.

6. ___ ___ ___ ___ she want a cat? ___ ___, she doesn't.

7. It's hot. Take ___ ___ ___ your ___ ___ ___ ___ ___ ___.

8. Where's your ___ ___ ___ ___ ___ ___ ___ ___ ___ ___ ___?

    He's in the kitchen with my father and brother. He ___ ___ cooking.

9. ___ ___ it a ___ ___ ___ ___ ___? Yes, it is a horse.

Mystery message:

47